How to get out of

Debt Permanently!

How to get out of Debt Permanently!

JOAN GIROUX

First Edition Published 2011 by Mentor Media 1759 Oceanside Blvd. Suite C-217, Oceanside, California

Published in the United States of America

ISBN: 978-0615580227 (Mentor Media)

Cover Design by pjsdesign

Dedicated to my late grandfather, Dean M. Snyder, Journalist - who encouraged my writing in the first decade of my life; and to my late father, Dean D. Snyder, Certified Financial Planner and mentor – who would have loved to see this work finally published.

About the Author

Joan Giroux dug herself out of debt and has helped others do the same for more than twenty years. She is passionate about helping ordinary people live extraordinary lives by learning to use money well.

Joan is a Certified Financial Planner and owns Money Mentors in Oceanside, California. She has been advising families and businesses about financial issues since 1983.

Table of Contents

Disclaimer

This book is presented solely for educational and entertainment purposes. Many of the financial concepts are in common use and have been presented in many forms in the past. This book is to serve only as a resource for you and your financial advisor when considering an appropriate financial plan for you individually. The author and publisher are not offering it as legal, accounting, or other professional services advice. While best efforts have been used in preparing this book, the author and publisher make no representations or warranties of any kind and assume no liabilities of any kind with respect to the accuracy or completeness of the contents and specifically disclaim any implied warranties of merchantability or fitness of use for any particular purpose. With financial planning, one shoe does not fit all. Therefore, this book may not necessarily set forth the best financial plan for you individually. Neither the author nor the publisher shall be held liable or responsible to any person or entity with respect to any loss or incidental or consequential damages caused by, or allegedly to have been caused by, directly or indirectly, the information or programs contained herein. No warranty may be created or extended by any sales representatives or written sales materials. Every individual and company is different and the advice and strategies contained herein may not be suitable for your situation. You should seek the services of a competent financial planning professional before beginning any financial self-improvement program. The examples, their characters, and entities are fictional. Any likeness to any actual persons, either living or dead, is strictly coincidental.

Acknowledgments

First and foremost, I thank God, my Creator, Redeemer, and Inspiration for my ability to write this book. I pray that those who read it be blessed with financial and spiritual prosperity.

I deeply appreciate my husband, Richard S. Giroux who keeps me grounded. I also want to thank my remarkable editor, Kalen R. Snyder of Editing4Everything.com; Shirley and Marco Gonzalez, translators; Corinne Jimenez, editor for the Spanish version; and last but not least my friends and family who have provided encouragement, ideas, and advice throughout the writing of this book – with special thanks to Richard Giroux, Kathryn Little, Malia Campbell, Wiley Jones, Becky Noel, Paula Snyder, Katy Valenzuela, and Dianne Warren.

Introduction

There are many lessons I have learned as a financial planner over the past thirty years. The most important ones are contained in this book.

If money (or lack thereof) has caused pain in your life, you have come to the right place. If you want to enjoy a prosperous future, this is the beginning of your journey.

I wrote this book with you in mind. Whether you know it or not, you have important work to complete in this life. Solid money skills will help you with this. My hope is this book will help to refresh your most useful skills and teach some new ones to help you now and in the future.

This book is designed so you can either read through the book to become familiar with the general concepts, or methodically work through it one chapter at a time implementing your own personal debt elimination plan.

1

The Cost of Living

B elieve it or not, money problems are among the easiest problems in the world to solve. Take health problems or relationship problems for example - they can be very complicated. But money problems are straightforward if you cut through the distractions and focus on simple dollars and cents.

Cash comes in and cash goes out month after month. Problems can arise when less money is coming in than going out over a period of time. When this happens for a prolonged period, we can find ourselves in debt and sometimes unable to meet the expenses of ordinary daily living. Whether you have a little debt or a lot, you will need some basic information to help you resolve the problem.

First, you will need to know what your expenses are. Don't guess. Take the time to look up what you have actually spent over the last year. Use your bank statements, credit card statements, check register, or any financial records you can access online. Gathering this data may be tedious – okay, it will be tedious – but it will be worth the effort. Believe me; I've already tried the shortcuts like guessing on one or two things rather than looking them up. If I thought this chore was unexciting the first time - it was absolutely wearisome when I had to do it over again because of some wrong guesses. Save yourself aggravation and do it right the first time. Set aside some time to do this when interruptions will likely be at a minimum. If you truly don't know how to perform this step or just can't stay motivated on your own, get someone to help you. Promise them a chocolate cupcake with sprinkles (or any other suitable bribe) if they help you out.

List every one of your individual expenses. Yes, every single one including those late night trips to the ice cream store and downloading those new tunes to your phone. Appendix A at the end of this book has worksheet models you can duplicate to help you with this. The worksheets are designed so you can list your expenses month by month. Knowing when expenses are due will help you when you reach Chapters Three and Five. There are computer software programs you can use as well. Some software programs will actually let you download your transactions from the bank right into the program and sort them into categories thus eliminating the need for the worksheets. In any event, don't make more work than is necessary by trying to learn a whole new software program to complete this task. The important thing is to get the job done. Learn what your expenses are, verify that those expenses are accurate, and move on to calculating your income.

If you use cash, begin saving receipts for each and every purchase you make. Make it simple for yourself. Carry a plastic bag (or other appropriate container) to keep your receipts in, sort them at the end of the month, and use the worksheet model in Appendix A to log these expenditures. It may take up to three months to have a true reflection of your actual spending but accuracy is important.

Here is a list of expenses to help trigger your memory:

Charitable Contributions / Tithe
Estimated Tax Payments
Mortgage Payment
Second Mortgage Payment
Rent
Home Owner Association Dues
Household Repairs
Home Maintenance
Gardening / Cleaning
Water
Waste Disposal / Trash
Gas
Electricity
Other Household Expenses
Vehicle Payment
Vehicle Fuel
Vehicle Insurance
Parking Fees / Tolls
Vehicle Maintenance / Repairs
License Plates / Registration Fees
Savings for Future Vehicle Purchase
Groceries
Eating Out
Other Food Expenses
Sundries / Toiletries
Clothing
Dry Cleaning
Medical / Dental Insurance Premiums
Prescriptions

Medical / Dental Co-payments
Dietary Supplements
Fitness Memberships
Other Medical / Health Expenses
Telephone
Internet / Cable Service
Other Communication Expenses
Postage
Subscriptions
Credit Card Payment
Spending Money
Haircuts / Grooming
Cosmetics / Services
Professional Services / Tax, etc.
Child Care
Allowances
Adult Support
Education / Tuition
Lessons
Pet Care
Entertainment / Movies
Recreation / Hobbies
Sporting / Theater Events
Summer Camp
Newspaper / Subscriptions
Membership Dues
Birthday Expenses
Holiday Expenses
Gifts
Vacations
Anniversary Expenses

Savings for Annual Expenses
Extra Payments to Creditors
Addition to Emergency Savings
Other Expenses

Next, using pay check stubs, tax or banking records, cal-culate the income you have taken home over the past year. Don't get sidetracked at this point by worrying about taxes or other deductions taken from your paycheck. To keep it simple, you want to know how much your take home pay is. It is important to note how often (for ex-ample every two weeks, every month, etc.) these sums of money are paid to you and are available to pay bills. If your income fluctuates a great deal throughout the year, it is especially important to note how much money was paid to you, how often it was paid, and the month in which you received it.

If you are paid in cash, you may need to begin keeping records of sums of money as you receive them and note how frequently you receive them.

Finally, add up all your expenses for the year. Add up all your income for the year. Subtract your expenses from your income. At this point, it doesn't matter whether your income or expenses are higher. Simply note these numbers and, if necessary, verify they are accurate. Accuracy is very important for your plan to work.

When you have finished this step, congratulate your-self. Open that bottle of bubbly you've been saving for a special occasion or indulge in that special (inexpensive) treat; do something nice for yourself. The most important part of your work is complete. Confirming your income and expenses is the most important step toward eliminating debt and achieving financial freedom.

Chapter Summary

- Gather any documents and online records you need to verify income and expenses (such as check register, bank or credit card statements, paycheck stubs, or purchase receipts).
- List all your expenses and verify their accuracy.
- List all your income and verify its accuracy.
- Subtract your expenses from your income to determine any surplus or shortfall.

2

The Power of Attitudes

N ow that you have some accurate numbers with which to
work, you may have some emotional reactions to these
numbers. You may feel surprise or discomfort. If you are ex-
periencing negative emotions over what you have just dis-
covered in Chapter One, please don't let that freeze you up.
You can't change the past. The facts are the facts. Financial
problems are fixable. By making a few adjustments to your
old attitudes and habits, you can free yourself from the bur-
den of debt – permanently! You are about to take control of
your money in a new way.

Let's take a look at three main culprits I have encoun-
tered which are particularly troublesome when managing
cash flow. I address them specifically because they are so
pervasive.

- Culprit Number One – Not being able to delay
  gratification

Having the ability to delay gratification is a valuable financial tool. We begin developing this skill as children and yet
many of us, even as mature adults, still struggle with con-
trolling our impulses. I am one of them. From my own

experience and what I have observed from clients, delayed gratification is learned by positive reinforcement. The only way I know to acquire enough positive reinforcement is through practice – a lot of practice. If you try something enough times and alter your behavior ever so slightly until you get the desired results, you will likely learn that gratification after some delay can be very sweet indeed.

Here is an example from my own life. From a young age, I have always had the ability to earn money. As a result, I didn't have to wait as long to make certain purchases as some of my peers who relied solely on their parents for income. Over time, I actually became a bit of an impulse buyer. When I was in my mid-twenties, one of my dearest friends moved 6,000 miles away. Neither of us had a lot of money nor the means to acquire it in the near future. I was devastated thinking how many years it would be before I would see her again. I was genuinely grief stricken. During this time, I happened to open my "junk" drawer in my kitchen. It was the drawer where I threw everything that really didn't seem to belong anywhere in particular. In it were dozens of various key chains, coin purses, and other small items. I had acquired most of them while standing in line at multiple stores. I would see something, think to myself, "Oh, that's cute", and then mindlessly toss the item on the counter with my other purchases. But this particular time I opened that drawer, it became apparent to me how much money I had wasted on needless purchases. If I could simply curb my impulse buying, the pennies I would save could turn into dollars.

I vowed right then and there I would stop wasting money on such useless items. Instead, I would set aside some money before I had the chance to spend it and save it for an airline ticket to go see my friend. It worked! Neither my income nor my expenses changed substantially, yet less than two years later, I had saved enough to make my first flight across the Atlantic to visit my friend.

I attribute my success to two factors. First, I had a reward in mind that was much more important to me than the temporary satisfaction of having something new. Second, I learned to ask myself two questions. "Do I need it?" If the answer was yes, I would ask myself a second question, "Can this purchase be postponed?" These two questions still serve me well in delaying gratification for the sake of a more rewarding goal.

For me, simply taking a quick moment to think through a purchase before I make it enables me to use my money more deliberately and wisely. It helps me consciously make a distinction between a true need I have and a simple desire I feel. I feel far less anxious about money, more satisfied with the purchases I do make, and generally happier with my life.

I encourage you to ask yourself these two questions before your next purchase. "Do I really need it?" And, "even if I do, can this purchase be postponed?" Make note of your honest answers and perhaps this little tip will work as well for you as it does for me.

Later in this chapter, you will see several specific ideas for cutting spending. These ideas may help you curb your spending as well.

- Culprit Number Two - Unexamined Attitudes and Expectations

Attitudes about money can be deeply rooted in us and have a powerful influence on our decisions. Some viewpoints may lead us to adopt unrealistic expectations for our finances.

We can choose to challenge what we believe, then incorporate our new ideas to craft new attitudes. As we learn and grow, we can modify our expectations to better suit our purposes.

The single most detrimental attitude toward finances that I have seen is what I call an "attitude of entitlement." Many of us have learned to measure our success materially by comparing ourselves with our peers or believing certain possessions are part of a basic standard of living. It is very dangerous to assume that we "should" have certain things in life. I have seen this attitude drive good people into severe debt and strain business, partnership, and marital relationships.

Let's examine the assumptions behind this attitude for a moment. This attitude is sometimes acquired from the very culture of our society. We tend to measure our value by where we live, what we drive, or how we dress. Yet, our genuine worth is not determined by how much stuff we own. Our true worth is measured by who we ARE not what we have. No one is born with the right to enjoy certain possessions. We come into this world with nothing but our bodies and we leave it with nothing but our spirits. Our possessions are simply for our use and enjoyment while we are here on earth. I believe this is why so many people strive for years to achieve monetary wealth then find severe disappointment at the end of that road. Don't get me wrong, wealth can be a wonderful thing. Prosperity is magnificent. But chasing after possessions to "measure up" to some arbitrary standard is a waste of time, energy, and money. There is a big difference between pleasure and happiness. We may get some pleasure from having new stuff, but it will not bring the joy we experience from using our unique talents to make our relationships and world a better place.

Consider what you hear, especially advertising slogans. A well-known and widely used advertising phrase encourages consumers to buy something because, "you deserve it." Think about this. When you hear this phrase, is someone giving you a gift or an award for something you have accomplished? The reality is you are exchanging your own hard earned cash for an item that may bring you *at best* some momentary pleasure. Accepting the idea "you deserve it" as truth is like accepting that using a specific deodorant brand will make you enormously attractive to the love of your life. Your worth and attractiveness come from somewhere far deeper within you than having some silly product from a store shelf. In our culture of relative wealth and materialism, some catch phrases have been so often repeated, that we can be tempted to incorporate them into our acceptable living standards with very little examination. I think if you hear a lie enough times, it starts to sound like the truth simply because it has become so familiar. But, there is a remedy.

Adopting an attitude of gratefulness is the antidote to an "attitude of entitlement." Recognizing what you have, cherishing it, and using it wisely are some of the best tools for success in finances and in life. This realization allows you to remain happy, yet focus your energies on learning and achieving what brings personal satisfaction. Because gratitude gladdens us, it helps boost our energy for cultivating our talents, relationships, and shaping a life full of meaning and purpose.

Attitudes have a profound impact on our ability to make wise decisions. Even when we are not consciously aware of them, our attitudes affect our emotions in a way that can't help but influence our choices. Taking the time to recognize what we have; our resources, our talents, and our blessings, enables us to build on those and move forward.

How do we develop and nurture an "attitude of gratitude?"

One way is to count our blessings on a regular basis. Acknowledge the resources you have. If you have a talent that enables you to earn money to live, be thankful. If you have good health, be thankful. If you have friends who add to your life, be thankful. You get the idea. Remember, this is about counting your own blessings, not comparing what you have with what others have. If you are the competitive sort and must compare, compare what you have with the possessions of those in third world countries. Many people in these parts of the world are grateful to have shoes so they can WALK (not drive) the miles required to reach necessary destinations.

Another way to nurture gratitude is to share what you have with others. If you have a closet full of clothes – donate the clothes you seldom if ever wear to those who can use them regularly. If you have packaged food and know you are unlikely to use it before the expiration date, donate it to a food bank. You might be surprised at how these simple actions nurture an "attitude of gratitude."

These sorts of exercises not only help build our character,

they actually help us make better financial choices. How do they help? First, they increase our awareness of reality. Dealing with factual reality is very helpful when making choices. Secondly, gratitude breeds joy and happy people tend to make better decisions overall in life. Decisions made out of bitterness or envy seldom turn out to be effective choices in the long run.

- Culprit Number Three - Thinking things "should" happen in a certain way or in a certain order

One of the obstacles many people experience is trying to live up to an unrealistic standard. We may have formed some expectations from a wide variety of false teachings and/or misconceptions. Some may come from ideas we learned growing up or standards that have been touted by people we admire. Regardless of the source, they almost always attack us at the core of our self-esteem. Unless we can think them through and correct our false impressions, we are bound to repeat the same mistakes. I've met many people who grew up in such a class conscious environment that they find it humiliating to shop in certain lower priced stores even when the quality of the merchandise is adequate. One of my friends will not consider buying anything used. I have run across countless people who are embarrassed to tell people their occupation, even when they are employed in perfectly legal and honorable though modest work. Without going into all the psychological elements that might be contributing here, I will suggest some coping mechanisms to help us use our money better.

Consider these concepts as a starting point.

Most of our discomfort about our lifestyle exists almost exclusively in our thinking. We can be perfectly comfortable physically in our existing surroundings, but miserable emotionally because we spend time and energy desiring what others seem to have, but we do not.

Adopt the idea that any work that is legal, moral, and provides a useful end product or service for others is honorable work. Develop a mature conscience and follow it. Family expectations, whether actual or perceived, can be a stumbling block – especially if those expectations require an outward show of apparent wealth. Give yourself permission to break the mold. Use your individual talents and skills to earn your living and live within your means. For support, surround yourself with companions who share your same values.

There is more than one "right" way to do things. Sometimes, we can become trapped by thinking we should do things a certain way or use a certain method to achieve our goals. For example, some may think they "should" balance their bank account to the penny each month. If that keeps you from becoming overdrawn or motivates you to save money, great! But, to balance your account just for the sake of balancing your account is not very meaningful. Focus on the result you want to achieve more than the method of getting there.

Chapter Summary
- Learning to delay gratification may help you better control your impulses and use money more deliberately.
- Adopting healthy attitudes and expectations about

your lifestyle enables you to worry less and make more satisfying choices.

• Realizing there are many "right" ways to do things can free you to work with your own personality and still use money responsibly.

3

Balancing Acts

Everyone I know has limited financial resources. I don't know anyone who has an unlimited pot of money somewhere that allows them to spend whatever they want whenever they want. Even my wealthiest clients have a finite amount of money.

Most of us occasionally (or frequently) experience short falls of cash and use credit cards or other debt to help see us through a tight spot. It becomes a problem when we have trouble making our payments and paying for the expenses of daily living. When this occurs, there are two obvious solutions. Either increase your income or decrease your expenses. There are a lot of ways to do both.

We'll start with decreasing expenses. Our basic needs consist of food, shelter, and clothing. If we don't have the option of walking to work and still need to earn a living, we need transportation too. When we have health issues, medical expenses may come into play as well. The list can go on and on. The difficulty many people have is distinguishing between actual *needs* and lifestyle *conveniences* that have become commonplace in our lives. To illustrate this point, I'll describe some common choices people face.

- Jack has worked two jobs since he graduated. He eventually wants a professional career but has not landed the job he wants due to the stressed economy and hiring freezes in his field. He has a truck payment and shares rent with a roommate. His other expenses are minimal except for student loans. His second job recently laid him off. He is now faced with lowering his expenses until he can find additional work. He just deferred his student loan payments and successfully negotiated his interest rate on his credit card to lower his monthly payments. He is looking hard at his other expenses to see what else he might be able to cut. Changing his mobile phone plan to one that costs less is one thing he can consider, but he has a two-year contract with penalties if he ends the contract early. Borrowing money from his family or friends is not an option as they are also strapped financially.

Possible Solutions:

- He could consider finding a place to live with lower rent or get an additional roommate.
- He could shop more carefully for groceries and gasoline to cut costs.

Can you think of any other areas he can lower expenses? What would you do in his position?

Here is another example to get those creative juices flowing.

- Mark and Cleo have been married for six years and

have two children under the age of 4. They both earn good incomes and bought a home two years ago with a variable interest rate mortgage. They have no other debt and live somewhat frugally in order to afford their home. Recently their mortgage interest rate increased and their house payment nearly doubled. They have tried to refinance their home unsuccessfully. The housing market would not fetch them a price for their home that would even pay off the current mortgage balance. They recently sold one car and have begun sharing their other vehicle and using public transportation to reduce costs. They also eliminated their internet package at home and have opted to use the local library for their internet needs and to check out books and movies for entertainment. They are very selective about who cares for their children while they are at work and are not willing to change child care providers; nor is their provider willing to reduce her bill.

Possible Solutions:

- They might begin cooking from scratch rather than buying prepared foods to save money on groceries.
- They might also consider having a good friend or relative move in with them and pay rent to increase their income.

What else might they do? What would you do?
Here is one more very typical scenario.

- June aged 58, is a recent widow with two grown children who have only recently begun their own careers and families. Her income was reduced substantially when her husband passed away. She has successfully reduced her expenses, lives extremely frugally, and has no debt whatsoever. She has a high school education and no recent work experience, but is very willing to work. She recently got copies of several books to help her determine her skills and their potential value in the workplace. She has been taking temporary part time work through an employment agency. Her biggest dilemma is obtaining health insurance as her coverage will expire in less than a year and she will not be covered by Medicare for several more years. Her desire is to find a full time job with health benefits and a retirement plan as she has very little money in savings. She makes a point of telling everyone she meets that she is looking for work. She has joined a women's resource group in her community that provides mutual support for its members.

Potential Solutions:

- She might consider selling her home and paying cash for a smaller residence. Smaller homes typically have lower maintenance costs as well.
- She might join an organization that could help her qualify for group health insurance, or join a cost sharing health plan at a reduced cost.

What else could she do? What would you do?

Just as the cases above illustrate, many people begin trying to cut expenses by looking at their largest expenses. This can be very effective, but here are some subtle changes people can make to cut expenses as well.

You may or may not have tried some of these ideas yourself. Here is a list that has worked well for others.

Plan your meals for the week around what is already in your cupboards and refrigerator.

Compare prices and shop selectively.

Buy only items that you need.

Make a list and buy only what is on the list.

Don't shop for groceries when you are hungry.

Use coupons and watch for sales to reduce costs. Be careful with coupons and sales though. Don't let them lure you into buying items you wouldn't use normally just because items are offered at a lower price.

Before setting out to shop and run errands, route your stops to save time and fuel. If necessary, take an empty ice chest or insulated bag to keep cold groceries from spoiling while you finish your errands.

Don't entertain yourself by shopping unless you are very disciplined. Or, leave your means to pay for something at home. Be willing to go home to retrieve your debit or credit card if you see a purchase you really want to make.

Be careful with catalogues and browsing on the internet to shop. If you don't know an item exists, you will not be tempted to buy it. This doesn't mean you can't shop on the internet for *needed* items at lower prices, but avoid browsing for the sake of browsing. When shopping with catalogues or the internet, consider shipping costs when comparing prices.

Plan your wardrobe carefully. While you are trying to limit spending, buy or replace only what you absolutely need to clothe yourself in a functional and appropriate manner. Choose clothing that will outlast fashion trends. Search for well-made clothing that fits you well. Clothing that is too small will not last as long as clothing that fits properly. Tight fitting items stress seams, zippers, and other fasteners.

Take care of your clothing. Follow laundering instructions to help clothing last longer. Learn how to mend or find someone to mend clothing for you.

Take care of your shoes. Regular cleaning and proper storage can help them last longer.

Shop at thrift stores or trade clothing with friends to expand or replace wardrobe items. This works especially well for children who outgrow their clothing quickly.

Choose where you buy fuel for your vehicle. Remain mindful of the difference between cash and credit prices – they do differ at some fuel stations.

Maintain your vehicle well. Recommended oil changes and other maintenance can go a long way in helping your vehicle remain reliable.

Talk with your insurance agent about coverage and premiums. Consider raising deductibles to keep premiums down. Reducing coverage is not always the best way to reduce costs since it might leave you vulnerable to legal action which can be very costly.

Learn new ways to entertain yourself that cost little or no money. Visit a nearby park and enjoy nature or people watching. Watching children and pets playing can be very entertaining. Rent movies from the library, or go to free community events such as concerts, plays, or school sporting events. Develop friendships with people who have similar financial situations and interests to your own.

If you have children, trade babysitting duties with other responsible parents to enjoy an outing without babysitting costs.

Go on a scavenger hunt in your own home for items you can use to make homemade gifts (rather than spending money on gifts).

Know yourself. If you're a spender by habit or nature, make yourself accountable to a friend who is not a spender. Cut up those credit cards or close the accounts if they are too tempting for you. Make a game out of saving money or cutting spending. You might give yourself points for dollars saved and subtract points for dollars spent over budget. Measure your progress periodically.

Look for self-employment opportunities. If you are good at sewing, carpentry, or some other skills, let people who live in senior communities know you are willing to help for a fee. Many elderly home bound people who have limited vision, might enjoy having you read to them. People who can no longer drive might be willing to pay you to take them shopping, to doctors' appointments, or even to run errands. (Check with your insurer if you will be driving people on a regular basis.) Students at local schools might benefit from your ability to tutor them on a subject. People with pets might be willing to pay you for taking care of their pets while they are away or walking their dogs if they are unable to do so themselves. Determine what activities you enjoy, then find someone who needs those services and is willing to pay a reasonable price for your help.

Chapter Summary

- Go through your expenses from Chapter One to see where you can cut expenses using some ideas from this chapter.
- Consider ways you might increase your income.
- Continue decreasing expenses and increasing income until you have at least some money left over.

4

When Two Heads Are Better than One

Sometimes it is necessary to make hard choices like giving up a residence for which you have a great emotional attachment or refusing to provide financial assistance for an adult child. When there are deep emotional ties that are affected by financial cuts, getting some sage advice may be in order. You might seek the help of a spiritual leader or professional counselor such as a psychologist or financial advisor. Getting advice from an objective yet compassionate expert can boost your confidence that you are making prudent decisions despite difficult circumstances.

Another situation that often calls for some wise outside counsel is when financial partners disagree. This is especially true in marriage. What one spouse does with money affects the other whether or not we like it. When disagreement leads to the relationship breaking down, very serious repercussions can result. Seventy percent of divorces among couples in their first marriage are attributed to money problems. When money runs low and emotions run high, counseling of some sort may ease the distress of solving marital money problems.

I am passionate about encouraging integrity in a marriage. A mediocre marriage can be revitalized and each partner can thrive when couples learn to solve problems as a team. I have been blessed with phenomenal success in helping couples resolve money issues AND strengthen their marriages. Every partnership has conflicts. How we resolve those conflicts results in either increased friction or increased well-being. Perhaps spouses can find some common ground from which to start solving money conflicts and eliminate their debt by using these tips.

- Spouses can each use different methods to achieve the same mutual purpose. Your partner does not have to do things exactly the way you do to be successful. Remember the part about thinking things "should" be done a certain way or in a certain order? Flexibility with *accountability* is the secret to success here. Decide on a mutual goal. Be honest with and accountable to one another. Allow your partner the freedom to do things their own way so long as the results are what you mutually agreed upon.

    For example: John blames Jane for spending too much on shoes. Jane blames John for spending too much on golf. John claims Jane wouldn't spend so much if she would just check their account balance before spending money. He further claims he has to play golf to get new business. Jane claims shopping with her sister is her only "real" emotional outlet. She further claims John plays golf more than half the time with people who will never become clients; he is using the new business claim as an excuse.

In situations such as this, the argument can stay indefinitely focused on how each partner is to blame. Emotions can escalate to a damaging level. The focus needs to change from blaming one another to coming up with mutually agreeable solutions to the problem.

RECOMMENDATION: This couple needs to refrain from issuing blame and focus on the core problem to work together on solutions. The core problem with Jane and John is not who is spending what. Rather, it is that they both need to spend less money. To do this they may come up with some mutually agreeable solutions to reduce spending. They might agree that putting $100 per month in a savings account and allocating an "allowance" for each of them to spend on shopping and golf will resolve the problem. Each party can achieve those goals by whatever reasonable methods they choose. Once per month, they can report back to one another how much money was added to the savings account and whether each partner kept their spending within budget. If mistakes were made, they can determine how behaviors will change to succeed in meeting the mutual goals.

- Treat each other with respect. When you speak, speak respectfully. Don't accuse, berate, or otherwise verbally attack your spouse. Refrain from name calling, foul language, or using sarcasm. If you are

exceptionally angry, calm yourself down before beginning any conversation. If you need a little extra
motivation, speak to your spouse as if you are speak-
ing to someone in your life who you deeply respect.
Remain aware of your tone of voice – keep it respect-
ful. If you don't think you can do this, please think
again. Have you ever had to answer an important
telephone call while you were angry about something
else? Does your tone change from "I CAN'T STAND
THIS ONE MORE SECOND" to "*Oh, hi. Thanks sooo
much for returning my call?*" I know I've pulled that
off more than once. At least try to make your tone
neutral if you can't make it pleasant.

When you listen, start with the assumption your spouse has
something valuable to share. Try to understand what your
partner is trying to communicate. Don't assume you know
what your spouse is about to say next – even if you think
you know. Listen to one another's concerns. Truly listen. DO
NOT interrupt one another unless the house or dog is on fire
(or some other equally extreme emergency). Interrupting
one another is rude and disrespectful. You will have your
chance to say your bit and ask clarifying questions when
your spouse has finished. Give each party a chance to voice
their concerns in about three minutes or less. Most of us
can't pay attention and remember well enough to respond
beyond three minutes. When it is your turn to speak, don't
make accusations; simply state your concerns and why a
certain behavior or idea worries you. Do not assume your
partner thinks like you. Be willing to explain your thinking
and reasons behind your concerns by stating facts without

placing blame. Help your spouse understand how you "connect the dots." Be willing to admit your part in the problem.

> For example: Jane overspent her "allowance" by $12. John states his concern that if this behavior continues, they will continue to have money problems. Jane rationalizes that it was such a small amount it shouldn't make that much difference. John listens without interrupting and **refrains** from accusing her of not keeping up her end of the bargain. When Jane has finished and it is his turn to speak, he states that if each of them overspends by even $5 per month they will not be able to meet their mutual goals. John holds Jane accountable and states that spending small amounts over the spending limit is not what they agreed. Jane admits this is true. She agrees to cut her allowance by $12 next month in order to continue working toward their mutual goals.

The communication skills you learn by working through money issues can and often do transfer to other sensitive areas of marriage. Sorting through money problems can teach valuable communication skills that help strengthen a marriage and your respect for one another.

- Don't surrender your personal responsibility for finances in your relationship and leave all financial issues to your partner. Each partner needs to play a part in making financial decisions. How you divide the tasks related to financial issues is up to you, but check in with one another at least three or four times a year to make sure you are meeting your mutual goals. What is inspected is respected. Healthy communication and trust can be built by working together as partners on financial issues.

Chapter Summary

- Mastering these three concepts can significantly decrease the friction in your relationship.
  - Allow your partner the freedom to do things differently than you would do them.
  - Behave respectfully and listen without interrupting.
  - Take personal responsibility for actively participating in financial decision making.
- Two heads really can be better than one. Recognize when professional help might help you resolve particularly tough financial issues and ease emotional distress.

5

Go with the Flow

C ash Flow that is. Cash flows in from income and out from expenses.

Once your income and expenses are adjusted so you can meet all your financial obligations, there is another thing that will help you pay your bills on time – anticipation. You will need to use some foresight to anticipate future expenses.

The following is a common cash flow problem I encounter with clients. People forget about expenses that are due only once a year like vehicle registration or membership dues. For someone living from pay check to pay check, this can be a real dilemma. Have you ever been in the situation where you thought all the bills that were due had been paid? Maybe you even had a little money left over. Then, you received a big fat bill you had forgotten was due at that time of year. That certainly has happened to me. We'll call that a cash flow glitch. This section is about minimizing those glitches.

Let me clarify a bit here. I'm not referring to unforeseeable expenses like paying airfare to travel to an unexpected funeral. We will address that later. Specifically, this section is to help you prepare to pay your bills on time by anticipating when they are due and setting aside money in advance to pay for them.

Some months you may have higher expenses than others. Perhaps December has more expenses for you due to holiday costs or cold weather heating bills.

In Chapter One you listed your expenses. If you used the worksheet in Appendix A, you may also have noted the months in which they were due. By preparing a Cash Flow Worksheet such as this, you are effectively creating a calendar to help you anticipate your expenses. This sort of Cash Flow Calendar can be updated and used year after year to prepare for forthcoming bills.

There are many ways to set aside the money for upcoming expenses. Here are some ideas.

Some people place cash in envelopes labeled with the specific purpose for which the money is intended. This is a simple method that works exceptionally well for people who aren't comfortable with bank accounts. Yet, it has some risks associated with it. Money can burn in a fire or it can be stolen. If you don't have strong self-discipline, you might be tempted to use it for things other than the intended purpose. I have seen this method work very well for many people and it is certainly a functional way to handle your cash flow if it appeals to you.

Some people prefer to keep a separate bank or savings account for just their quarterly and annual bills. After seeing what their annual expenses are, they simply set aside a certain amount each payday for these future expenses and draw from that account as the bills come due.

Other people are good at earmarking money for certain needs. They keep all their money in one account then review upcoming expenses regularly to make certain they are setting enough aside.

Perhaps you can come up with other methods as well. Whatever method you choose; it is important that it works for you. For most people, the simpler the method, the better.

Chapter Summary

- Review your expenses and the months they are due.
- Devise a method for setting aside money that will work for you.

6

Eliminating Debt

This is my formerly Secret Weapon - The 50/50 Rule of thumb for reducing and eliminating debt

This is the coup de grâce – the compassionate death blow, if you will - for debt. This is the core around which I build almost every debt reduction plan I write for clients. I have never seen it fail for anyone who has faithfully used it. It has worked for my clients for over twenty years in all kinds of economic conditions. No matter the interest rates, regardless of how savvy the client; it has worked.

This tool is *vital* when you have less money saved than that required to pay for a minimum of three to six-months expenses. Once you are debt free, you will want to set up and maintain an emergency savings account and replenish it on a regular basis. Imagine if you had the money for two years-worth of expenses set aside. That would afford you a lot of freedom in making your financial choices. For now though, we will work with having a goal of setting aside enough money to cover at least six months in expenses.

This 50/50 method requires that at least some money is left over after your necessary expenses are paid. If you have no money left after balancing income and expenses, you need to cut more expenses until you have some money left over. Then you can proceed with this plan.

Take a blank sheet of paper. In one column, write down all of your debt balances. By debt balance, I mean the total amount of money you owe each lender not the amount of your monthly payment. For example, you might pay Visa $125 per month but the total balance you owe is $7,500. So, you would write $7,500 in this column. Continue to list each of your debt balances. These might include your mortgage, vehicle loan balance, student loans, credit card balances, money owed to friends and family members – basically any money you owe to anyone. In the next column, write down the interest rate charged by that lender for that loan. In a third column, write down the minimum payment required by that lender each month. Leave the fourth new payment column blank for now. Here is a sample.

Lender	Balance Owed	Interest Rate	Min. Pay	New Pay
Mortgage	$375,000	5%	$2,013	
Visa	$7,500	8%	$125	
MasterCard	$1,500	14%	$30	
Totals			$2,168	

You will begin by working with the lender charging you the highest rate of interest. Interest rates can be negotiated with your lender and you may have some success in asking each of your lenders to lower the rate they are charging you. Often you can transfer your loan balances to a creditor offering a lower interest rate as well. Making phone calls to creditors can provide this information for you. If you want to negotiate interest rates here are some ideas that have worked for many of my clients.

- Before you call, decide how much you can afford to pay that individual lender. You may be asked to make a higher payment if given a lower interest rate.
- Ask to speak with someone who has the authority to negotiate payment and interest terms. Politely ask to speak with a supervisor if you lack the cooperation you expect.
- Ask for the lowest interest rate your creditor can provide.
- Be honest with your creditors about why you are trying to negotiate these terms. In my experience, credit representatives are so accustomed to being told lies they might assume you too are lying. Don't take it personally. If you have trimmed your budget as far as you can, it may help to be willing to send them your expenses and intentions in writing.
- Hold on to your self-esteem. The person on the other end of the phone is not superior to you. They are human just like you with a job to do. They may have learned to speak in a gruff and intimidating manner simply because they have to deal with tough people and situations so frequently.
- If you need time to think about the terms they offer you, say so and agree to a time you will call them

to respond. Don't feel pressured to make a decision right then and there.

- If you have a hard time staying motivated to make these calls, remember these calls may result in your saving many hundreds of dollars in interest.

After your negotiations and balance transfers, we will focus on the lender with the highest interest rate.

Determine the amount of money you have left over after all your required expenses are paid. Let's say you have $100 left over. Divide that number in half. You will be using half that money ($50) to create or add to an emergency savings account. (Remember, the goal is to have enough money in emergency savings to cover six months-worth of expenses.) The other half ($50) will be paid in addition to your minimum payment on your highest interest rate debt.

Lender	Balance Owed	Interest Rate	Min. Pay	New Pay
Mortgage	$375,000	5%	$2,013	
Visa	$7,500	8%	$125	
MasterCard	$1,500	14%	~~$30~~	$80
Totals			~~$2,168~~	$2,218

Let's use Sheila's numbers above as an example. Sheila currently has no emergency savings. She has a mortgage balance of $375,000 at an interest rate of 5%. Her minimum monthly payment is $2,013 per month. She also has two credit cards and owes balances on them. Her VISA card has a balance of $7,500, an interest rate of 8%, with a minimum payment of $125 per month. Her MasterCard has a balance of $1,500, an interest rate of 14%, with a minimum payment of $30 per month. Sheila has $100 to work with. She determined this by accurately calculating her income and expenses and determining how much money she had left after paying all her expenses. She will place $50 into savings. She will then apply the other $50 to the MasterCard debt for a total monthly payment of $80 (the original $30 minimum payment plus $50 extra). She will continue to make these payments until the second card has a zero balance and is completely paid. Each month she continues to put $50 into her savings account.

Let's take this a step further. Twelve months after Sheila initiates her plan, her car breaks down and she is faced with a repair bill of $450. She currently has a little over $600 in savings ($50 times 12 months plus the interest it earned). Rather than charge the car repair and increase her debt, she uses $450 from her savings to pay the bill and continues saving and paying down her debt.

Six months later, her second credit card has a zero balance and she has $80 more per month free to use. (That $80 had been used to pay her first credit card bill.) What does she do with that money? She adds it to her left over money at the end of the month, $50 currently going into savings plus $80 for a total of $130. She continues to employ the 50/50 rule. One half of the $130 ($65) will now go into savings and she will add the other $65 to her next highest interest rate debt which is her VISA card. She will now pay $190 (the minimum payment of $125 plus $65) toward her VISA card and continue saving $65 per month. Here is a sample.

Lender	Balance Owed	Interest Rate	Min. Pay	New Pay
Mortgage	$375,000	5%	$2,013	
Visa	$7,500	8%	$125	$190
~~MasterCard~~	~~$1,500~~	~~14%~~	~~$30~~	~~$80~~
			~~$2,168~~	~~$2,218~~
Totals				$2,203

One year later, Sheila receives the sad news that her be-loved uncle died. She is faced with travel expenses of $300 to attend the funeral. Fortunately, she now has a little over $1,200 in her savings. She pays her travel expenses from savings and continues with her regular debt reduction and savings payments.

Six months later, Sheila learns her beloved uncle has left her an inheritance of $5,000. Following the 50/50 rule, what will she do with it? Sheila again divides any extra money (in-cluding this $5,000 windfall) in half. Half ($2,500) goes into her savings account which is added to her existing balance of $1,350. This now gives her over $3,800 in savings. She uses the other $2,500 to pay down her current VISA leaving her with a much smaller VISA balance of $680 remaining. Continuing in this way, she will be free of credit card debt in about three months and she will have just over $4,000 in savings.

Now you may ask the question, "Could I pay off the whole debt with the inheritance and just be done with it?" or "Can I divide the money up differently, like 1/3 toward savings, 1/3 toward debt and 1/3 toward something else?" The answer is, of course you can – it's your money. But that isn't what Sheila did. The main reason this method works is because it breaks the cycle of debt. You cannot break the cycle of debt without simultaneously saving. Please let me repeat that because it is very important. *You cannot break the cycle of debt without simultaneously saving.* If you have nothing to fall back on when a car repair, funeral expense, or other unexpected expense occurs; you will just continue to dig yourself deeper and deeper into debt. It doesn't matter if savings interest rates are low and credit interest rates are high. Real life throws us curves. Unexpected expenses occur. Without savings, the usual recourse we have is to borrow more money which then leads us into a rapid downward spiral of increasing debt. Increasing debt can lead to anxiety that negatively affects many different aspects of our lives. On the other hand, taking steps and realizing progress in resolving money problems increases our self-confidence and our well-being.

There is another glitch which occasionally happens. If an unexpected expense occurs when you have just started saving, you may not have enough in your savings account yet to cover it. Perhaps a car repair is $450 and you only have $200 in savings. Use the $200 from savings and borrow or charge the balance of $250 to your lowest interest rate credit card. Then continue with your 50/50 plan. Eventually, your savings will increase and you will eliminate your debt.

By using this 50/50 approach you form the essential

habit of saving. It may take some time for you to form new habits such as setting aside money without being tempted to spend it on other things, particularly if your old habits are well entrenched. When you learn that paying yourself is just as important as paying your other bills, savings becomes more automatic and less difficult.

I will add one other possible approach here. Some people may benefit from paying down their smaller balances first. While paying down your highest interest rate debt first is the most effective mathematically, the psychological benefit of paying off a debt or two completely is valid if it helps keep you motivated.

Chapter Summary
- Paying extra money over minimum payments will eliminate debt more quickly.
- Paying your debt with the highest interest rate first will speed this process.
- Accumulating adequate savings breaks the cycle of debt.
- Using a planning tool, such as the 50/50 method, systematically helps eliminate debt *and* accumulate adequate savings.

7

The Realities of Daily Life

N ow that the mathematical and factual part of your plan is crafted, it's time to incorporate it into your daily life. This requires paying attention to the cash flow calendar you created with your worksheets in Chapter Five. You may need to update it periodically as income and expenses change. Expect that updating your cash flow information will be part of the ongoing maintenance of a successful plan.

It is helpful to keep your financial information somewhat organized. Choose a safe place for keeping your financial documents, such as checks and bills, until you process them. My husband and I keep ours in a container near where we open our mail. When we carry in the mail, we place our bills and important paperwork in a basket. By doing this, either of us can locate the necessary paperwork when we pay the bills. If your bills are scattered throughout your home, some may get overlooked. Placing your bills in the same place consistently minimizes the chance of this happening.

Decide when and how you will deposit money into your account. Automatic deposits are great if you can manage them. If you need to manually deposit checks, don't procrastinate. When you receive income, deposit it within three days or less. Set some ground rules for yourself.

Pay your bills at least once a month. Ideally, pay them on the same day of every month. Just make it a habit. For many people, paying bills as soon as they are received works well too. Whether you pay them electronically online or send checks or money orders, make sure you send the payments several days before they are due. Late charges are a waste of money, so avoid them by paying before the due date.

If you ever need to pay a bill late, inform your creditor. Working with your creditors can help decrease late charges and excess interest.

I didn't promise this process would be entirely painless. There will be times you need to perform unpleasant tasks, but your efforts will help ensure you don't encounter the same problems repeatedly over the rest of your life. As long as you have debt you remain a slave to your debtors.

Remember, this is about getting out of debt *permanently*. Forming new habits generally takes time. You might make some mistakes along the way. That's okay. Aim for progress not perfection. Learning and perfecting solid money skills enables you to solve new problems or challenges as they arise. As you experience financial success, your self-confidence will increase. Eventually, your new habits will become second nature and serve you well for a lifetime.

Finally, continue to grow your savings. This really is the essential key to achieving financial freedom and remaining permanently out of debt. Ultimately, you will want to have enough saved that you can choose to stop working and be able to live from your investments and any other pensions or annuities you may have.

Until this point, your goal has been to acquire enough money in savings to be able to pay six months-worth of expenses. When your debt is completely paid, you will have more money to save for future goals; like your next vehicle, that cabin in the woods, an education for your children, or retirement. Free of debt, you have the ability to accumulate and live completely from your own wealth. That can be an enormously freeing experience.

Your nest egg can really begin to grow when you are free of debt payments. Here is an example.

Sheila's debt payments originally totaled $2,168 per month. She continued using the 50/50 plan. After four years, she had acquired more than enough in her emergency savings account. As a result, she decided to add another $300 per month to her mortgage payments. Eighteen years later, she was completely debt free *with* her mortgage paid in full. Having freed up over $2,000 per month from debt payments, she then decided to place $2,000 per month in an account for retirement. By age 67, Sheila was still completely free of debt and had accumulated well over one million dollars*(*earning an average annual rate of eight percent over twenty years). Sheila never changed careers, or had significant promotions or raises, other than cost of living raises. Simply by paying down debt and continuing to save, Sheila became a millionaire and was able to enjoy a very comfortable retirement.

Chapter Summary
- Keep your financial paperwork organized.
- Form habits of depositing money and paying your bills in a timely manner.
- Continue to save and update your goals as your life circumstances change.

FAQ (Frequently Asked Questions)

**How do I get my partner and children to willingly partici-
pate in my debt reduction plan?**

Getting them to help in the planning process helps edu-
cate your family members about solving money problems. It also helps them take ownership when they have
actively participated in the decision making about spending
cuts. For example, cutting out allowances without warning
might cause resentment. But, letting the family choose to
lower their allowances and cut back on some grocery treats
might result in a much more agreeable outcome.

Occasionally, you will have family members who resist
making changes of any kind. If their behaviors are negatively affecting your health and well-being you may have
to set some hard limits with them. If you have trouble doing this, I highly recommend reading two books. One is
"Boundaries" by Henry Cloud and John Townsend. The
other is "Crucial Conversations" by Patterson, Grenny,
McMillan and Switzler. Some of the advice found in these
books may help you set healthy limits.

**Can refinancing my existing debt help and will it affect my
credit rating?**

One way to reduce your debt more quickly is to lower the

interest rate you are being charged. You can call your creditor and simply ask them to lower it, or you can find another lender who is willing to let you transfer your balance to them and repay it at a lower rate. Keep in mind that frequent switching of loans, credit cards, and mortgages can lower your credit score. But, my feeling about credit scores is this – if you take the necessary steps to handle your finances well, your credit score will eventually take care of itself. In my opinion, far too much importance has been placed on credit scoring. I am not disputing that a credit score will influence your ability to borrow money. I am simply suggesting that to achieve financial freedom, your credit score is probably less important than some other factors like prudent cash flow planning. Credit scores are unimportant unless you need to borrow money. Ideally, you will eventually be living completely off your own wealth, however modest that wealth might be.

Minimizing spending during holiday seasons is very difficult in my family. We have always exchanged gifts and I am expected to participate. What can I do to change their expectations of me?
Be honest. Reassure them that you want to participate in making holidays special. Tell them you have committed to changing your financial habits and that your resources are limited. They don't need to know details. Find creative ways to let them know you care about them.

What is "good debt?" I have heard certain kinds of debt are okay.
Good debt commonly refers to things like student or

business loans where taking on debt may increase the like-lihood of improving your income. I encourage people to use their own good judgment here. Any time you take on debt you are increasing the risk to your financial well-being. Investigate your choices between taking a loan, obtaining grant money, or waiting to pursue a project until you have enough money saved. Then, make an informed choice. Debt isn't necessarily bad; it is just risky because you are placing your financial well-being in another's hands so to speak.

I currently tithe (give 10% of my income) to my church. I am having trouble making my debt payments. Should I decrease my contributions?
I am a firm believer in tithing. I believe everything we have is a gift from God – even our ability to work hard to earn a living. I have experienced first-hand how tithing helps us retain an attitude of gratitude and reminds us to use our limited resources prudently. Plenty of wise advice can be found in Scripture. My favorite is Malachi 3:10. How much of your time, talent, and treasure (money) you choose to give is a personal choice to be made with an informed con-science. Only you can decide what is best in your circum-stances. Personally, I have chosen to continue tithing even when my financial circumstances were quite dire and have been successful at overcoming debt by other means, such as those suggested in this book.

I have paid off our debt time and time again, but my partner keeps getting us back in debt. How can I protect myself?
I am going to make the assumption you have already tried

reasoning with and educating your partner without success. Part of the answer depends on why your partner keeps running up debt. If the debt is due to lack of self-discipline in using credit cards or the like, investigate how you can close or limit certain credit accounts and limit your partner's ability to obtain monies allocated for living expenses. If the cause of irresponsible spending is due to a substance abuse, gambling problem or such, some professional counseling is probably in order. If your partner won't go; I recommend you go by yourself. Please consider reading "Boundaries" by Henry Cloud and John Townsend as well.

If you had only one piece of advice for prosperity what would it be?
View money as a tool not a goal. Integrity is the key to prosperity not money.

SUMMARY

In the beginning of this book, I told you I wrote it with you in mind. I wrote each chapter hoping I could convey one or two ideas that would help you use money to enhance your life. Thank you for investing your time to read it.

Here is a summary of the ideas presented.

The basic steps to construct a debt elimination plan:

- Gather accurate information about your income and expenses.
- Remain aware of your attitudes and how they affect your spending choices.
- Increase your income or reduce your expenses until you have at least some money left over.
- Employ the 50/50 plan of simultaneously saving and paying down debt.
- Continue to review your finances and savings regularly to successfully achieve your goals.

Key points to remember -

- Solid money skills will help you achieve success in many areas of your life.
- When you use accurate information about income and expenses, all money problems are solvable.
- Money resources are limited. Consciously choose how you use yours.

- Don't be afraid to ask for help when you need it.
- Accountability to a partner or friend can help keep you on track.
- Make savings a habit. Saving is the key to financial freedom.

Congratulations on investing in your financial education. I am praying for your successful journey toward prosperity.

APPENDIX A

Following are the Cash Flow and Debt Elimination work-sheets. You can duplicate these worksheets for your own use by drawing them on a piece of paper or using a spreadsheet program on your computer.

Cash Flow Worksheet	January	February	March
Income			
Income			
Total Income			
Expense			
Expense			
Expense			
Expense			
Expense			
Total Expenses			

Cash Flow Worksheet	April	May	June
Income			
Income			
Total Income			
Expense			
Expense			
Expense			
Expense			
Expense			
Total Expenses			

Cash Flow Worksheet	July	August	September
Income			
Income			
Total Income			
Expense			
Expense			
Expense			
Expense			
Expense			
Total Expenses			

Cash Flow Worksheet	October	November	December
Income			
Income			
Total Income			
Expense			
Expense			
Expense			
Expense			
Expense			
Total Expenses			

Debt Elimination Worksheet				
Lender	Balance Owed	Interest Rate	Min. Pay	New Pay
Totals